GARETH STEVENS
VITAL SCIENCE
Earth Science

ROCKS AND FOSSILS

by Richard Hantula
Science curriculum consultant: Suzy Gazlay, M.A.,
science curriculum resource teacher

GARETH**STEVENS**
GS
PUBLISHING
A Member of the WRC Media Family of Companies

Please visit our Web site at: www.garethstevens.com
For a free color catalog describing Gareth Stevens Publishing's
list of high-quality books and multimedia programs, call
1-800-542-2595 (USA) or 1-800-387-3178 (Canada).
Gareth Stevens Publishing's fax: (414) 332-3567.

Library of Congress Cataloging-in-Publication Data

Hantula, Richard.
    Rocks and fossils / Richard Hantula.
       p. cm. — (Gareth Stevens vital science - earth science)
    Includes bibliographical references and index.
    ISBN-13: 978-0-8368-7765-6 (lib. bdg.)
    ISBN-13: 978-0-8368-7876-9 (softcover)
    1. Rocks—Juvenile literature. 2. Minerals—Juvenile literature.
    3. Fossils—Juvenile literature. I. Title.
    QE432.2.H36   2007
    552—dc22   2006033117

This edition first published in 2007 by
Gareth Stevens Publishing
A Member of the WRC Media Family of Companies
330 West Olive Street, Suite 100
Milwaukee, WI 53212 USA

This edition copyright © 2007 by Gareth Stevens, Inc.

Produced by White-Thomson Publishing Ltd.
Editor: Walter Kossmann
Designer: Clare Nicholas
Photo researcher/commissioning editor: Stephen White-Thomson
Gareth Stevens editorial direction: Mark Sachner
Gareth Stevens editor: Leifa Butrick
Gareth Stevens art direction: Tammy West
Gareth Stevens production: Jessica Yanke and Robert Kraus

Science curriculum consultant: Tom Lough, Ph.D., Associate Professor of Science Education,
Murray State University, Murray, Kentucky

Illustrations by Peter Bull Art Studio
Photo credits: CORBIS, pp. 8 (© Reuters), 17l (© Fritz Polking, Frank Lane Picture Agency,
17r (© Steve Kaufman), 33 (© Francis Latreille), 37 (© Denis Scott), 39 (© Louie Psihoyos),41
(© Jonathan Blair), 45 (© Richard T. Nowitz); Ecoscene, p. 4; David Frazier, p. 36; Geoscience,
pp. 5 (both), 6 (all), 15t (all), 26; I-Stock, pp. 9, 10, 11, 12, title page and 14, 15b, 18, cover and 19,
20, 23, 24, 28, 29, 30, 31, 32 (both), 35.

Cover: The Colorado River eroded the soft rock and soil around this formation to create
a spectacular horseshoe bend.
Title page: While sandstone can be found in many regions of the United States, some of
the most picturesque formations are located in northern Wyoming.

Printed in Canada

1 2 3 4 5 6 7 8 9 10 10 09 08 07 06

TABLE OF CONTENTS

1 ROCKS AND MINERALS

All rocks are solid and hard, but they come in an amazing variety of sizes, shapes, colors, and textures. They are all composed of mixtures of materials, usually (but not always) including substances called minerals. Some are made almost entirely of one mineral.

Limestone is an example. It is composed mainly of the mineral calcite. Most rocks, however, are mixtures of two, three, or more minerals.

▼ A granite boulder sits in an unusual position on top of another rock formation in Yosemite National Park, California.

The word *mineral* is sometimes used for all sorts of substances. For example, many vitamin pills contain not only vitamins but also minerals. Workers in the mining industry often use the word *mineral* for any material taken from the earth. They may call oil, gravel, coal, and copper ore minerals.

The term *mineral*, however, is usually used more narrowly by scientists who study Earth and its rocks. These experts are known as geologists. For geologists, a mineral is a solid substance made of one or more simple chemicals called elements. Each element has its own specific type of atoms. Atoms are particles that constitute the building blocks of matter. In each mineral, atoms are combined in a particular way. They form a regular pattern called a crystal. Many geologists insist on one more thing before they call a substance a mineral. They require that it not be formed from living things.

Mineral Medley

More than four thousand minerals have been discovered on Earth. Color, hardness, and weight are some of the ways in which they differ. A key reason that minerals differ is that they are made of different elements. That is not the only reason, however. How the elements'

atoms are arranged in a crystal is also important. Combining the same atoms in different ways will produce different crystals, and the results will be different minerals. For example, atoms of carbon that are joined together in one way make diamond. Putting them together in a different way makes graphite. Graphite is black and quite soft. Diamond is transparent and is the hardest substance found in nature.

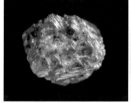

▲ Both diamond *(left)* and graphite *(right)* are made of carbon, but they are very different minerals. Graphite is soft, is black or gray in color, and has a metallic sheen. Diamond, formed under high pressure and temperature, is extremely hard.

A few minerals are plentiful in Earth's crust. This rocky top layer, especially the portion under the continents, is the part of the planet we know best. More than 98 percent of the continental crust is made up of just eight elements. The most common ones are oxygen and silicon. Minerals containing these two elements are found almost everywhere. One mineral, feldspar, makes up more than half of the continental crust. Feldspar is actually a group of related minerals. All feldspars contain not only oxygen and silicon but also aluminum plus another element. Quartz is the next most common mineral. It is silicon dioxide. The name means it is made up of two atoms of oxygen for every atom of silicon.

Prized Minerals

Gemstones are minerals that can be cut and polished to have an attractive look. They are durable and highly prized. After they are cut and polished, they are known as gems. Gems tend to be valued highly because they are not only beautiful but also so hard that they resist being scratched. Diamonds are the hardest of all, and they are especially prized. Beautiful, durable, and rare gemstones, such as emeralds and rubies, are said to be precious. Gemstones that meet only one or two of these three criteria are usually known as semiprecious.

▼ Two of these four gemstones, ruby *(upper left)* and sapphire *(upper right)*, consist primarily of the hard mineral known as corundum. Ruby's red color comes from the presence of a small amount of chromium. Green emerald *(lower left)* is made mainly of the mineral beryl. Topaz *(lower right)* tends to be white or light-colored.

Jade and zircon are examples of semi-precious stones.

Ores make up another group of prized minerals. An ore contains a valuable metal or another substance. For a mineral to be called an ore, it must be present in one place in amounts, or deposits, large enough to make mining worthwhile.

Nonmineral Rocks

While most rocks on Earth contain minerals, as defined by geologists, some do not. Coal is one example. It is a rock that was formed from the remains of dead plants. Two more examples are obsidian and pumice, which come from volcanoes. They are glassy and lack a crystal pattern.

Popular Gemstones

Scientists often rate the hardness of minerals on a scale from 1 to 10 called the Mohs scale. Here is a list of some of the best-known gemstones. It is arranged according to their Mohs hardness, starting with diamond, the hardest natural material.

Gemstone	Mohs Hardness
diamond	10
ruby	9
sapphire	9
topaz	8
emerald	7.5–8
garnet	6.5–7.5
zircon	6–7.5
opal	5.5–6.5
turquoise	5–6

Everyday Minerals

Minerals are all around you. Here are a few examples of items you might find in the bathroom and the minerals and similar materials they contain.

dandruff shampoo	coal tar, lithium clays, selenium
drinking glass	feldspar, silica, soda ash
lipstick, other makeup	clay, mica, talc, limestone, petroleum products
mirror	feldspar, silica, silver
talcum powder	talc and mica
tiles	clay, feldspar, wollastonite, talc, mineral pigments
toothpaste	fluorite, barite, calcite

2 ROCK TYPES

There are three basic types of rocks—igneous, sedimentary, and metamorphic. Each type is formed in a different way. A rock's makeup reflects the way it was formed. Rocks also carry other clues about their history. These clues may reveal when a rock was formed. They may also give hints as to what conditions were like when the rock was formed. There may even be clues about events that have occurred right up until the present. Clues found in rocks can help scientists learn about the history of Earth.

▼ Many scientists doubt that the traces of life said to be found in a meteorite from Mars in 1996 were actually made by Martian life-forms. The debate, however, continues. In 2001, an electron microscope view of the meteorite *(bottom)* revealed a chain of tiny magnetic crystals resembling the kind made by certain bacteria on Earth *(top)*.

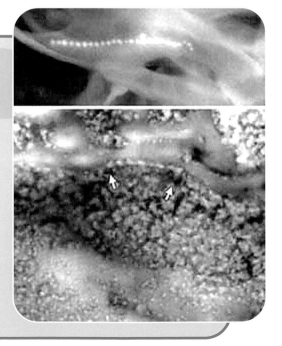

Signs of Life?

Meteorites are rocks that come from space. They help scientists learn about conditions in other parts of the solar system. They also carry clues about what things were like when the solar system was being formed. A few meteorites came originally from the planet Mars. In 1996, scientists found in one of them what looked like traces left by a tiny living creature! Other scientists said that the traces were probably made by other causes. Spacecraft exploring Mars may someday learn for sure whether life ever existed there.

Igneous Rocks

Most rocks in Earth's crust are igneous. They began as hot liquid material called magma. Magma usually is found at depths where it is much hotter than on the surface. This heat is how igneous rocks got their name. *Igneous* comes from a Latin word that means "fire." If magma gets cool enough, it turns solid and becomes igneous rock.

There are many kinds of igneous rocks. Each type is determined by how it was formed. Another factor is what its original magma was made of.

Intrusive Igneous Rocks

If magma cools slowly, it turns into one type of igneous rock. This can happen when magma moves to a part of the crust with a somewhat lower temperature. For example, magma might be pushed closer to the surface through a crack. The magma intrudes, or inserts itself, into the crack. The new rock that forms when the magma cools is called intrusive rock. Since the magma cools slowly, there is plenty of time for crystals to grow. As a result, the crystals in intrusive rocks tend to be large.

Although formed underground, some intrusive rocks later end up on the surface. If you look at such a rock, you can see in it large bits or particles called grains, which contain one or more crystals. The most common sort of intrusive rock on the surface is granite. It contains feldspar and quartz, along with a little mica and tiny bits of other minerals. It is very hard. Its color tends to be gray or whitish, but some kinds are pinkish or even other colors. The colors depend on the minerals that make up the granite. Another common intrusive rock, gabbro, is darker in color.

▲ This towering rock face in Yosemite National Park in California is made of granite. It was formed by intrusion of magma, which solidified and later was left behind when surrounding rock was worn away.

Extrusive Igneous Rocks

If magma cools down fast, it turns into a different type of igneous rock. This happens when magma comes out onto the surface. It may come out through an opening called a vent in a volcano. It may also come through a crack, or fissure, in the ground. Magma that flows onto the surface is called lava. The temperature on the surface is much lower than in the crust, and the lava cools quickly. Since the magma is pushed out, or extruded, onto the surface, igneous rocks made in this way are called extrusive. They are also sometimes called volcanic rocks. Extrusive rocks tend to have tiny grains. If they cool very quickly, they may even lack grains. They may look smooth like glass.

The most common extrusive rock is basalt. It is dark-colored. Its ingredients

▲ A highway passes by the edge of a rock formation of hardened lava.

are similar to those of the intrusive rock gabbro, but basalt and gabbro look different. It is much easier to see grains or crystals in gabbro. Because basalt comes from fast-cooling lava, its grains are very tiny. Many of the rocks brought back to Earth from the Moon are basalt. They were probably formed in the same way

Father of Geology: James Hutton

Scottish-born James Hutton (1726–1797) studied medicine but never worked as a doctor, instead pursuing an interest in rocks. Because of his discoveries and ideas, he is sometimes called the Father of Geology. He put forth the principle of "uniformitarianism," which holds that the processes shaping Earth have always been more or less the same. According to Hutton, processes such as erosion and volcanic eruptions occurred in the past much as they do today. He proposed, therefore, that major geologic change takes place slowly and that Earth is very old. Hutton studied volcanoes and showed that extrusive and intrusive rocks are igneous. He also came up with the principle of the rock cycle (see Chapter 3).

as Earth's basalt rocks—lava poured out onto the surface from below and cooled.

Another sort of extrusive rock is rhyolite. It is light-colored and has the same minerals as the intrusive rock granite. When certain kinds of lava cool very

▲ The so-called Giant's Causeway on the coast of Northern Ireland consists of thousands of columns of basalt that were formed some 60 million years ago when an extrusive lava flow quickly cooled.

Putting Igneous Rocks to Work

Since ancient times, people have made buildings and monuments from hard, durable granite. It can be polished, so it is also used as a decorative stone. Granite is often used today to make floor tiles and kitchen countertops.

Obsidian is shiny and sharp-edged. For ages, it has been used to make jewelry, mirrors, and cutting tools. Even today, doctors use obsidian scalpels because they are so sharp.

Lightweight pumice makes a good decorative stone. Ground-up pumice is an ingredient in some types of concrete. Pumice is an abrasive and is good for grinding, cleaning, or polishing surfaces. Pumice is also used to make cosmetics and soaps.

rapidly, the result is a glassy black or darkish rock called obsidian. Obsidian forms sharp edges when broken.

Sometimes lava contains air bubbles. It may seem like foam. If the lava is very thick, like molasses, the bubbles can't escape before it hardens into a rock. This rock is called pumice. It is full of sponge-like holes and is lightweight. Some kinds of pumice can even float on water.

Air also plays a role in another sort of igneous rock. Some volcanoes throw powdery dust, or ash, into the air. If the ash piles up, it may turn into a soft rock known as tuff.

Sedimentary Rocks

Most of the rocks on Earth's surface are sedimentary rocks. They were formed from sediment, or material that settles in an area. It might be sand, mud, dust, little stones, or the remains of dead plants and animals. The material may be deposited by water, wind, or even moving ice (as in a glacier). As more and more of the material piles up, its weight generates enormous pressure at the bottom of the sediment. Here the sediment material is squeezed tightly together and slowly turns into solid rock, a process that may take thousands, or even millions, of years.

Sediment sometimes settles on the seafloor. Sediment is also deposited on the bottoms of other bodies of water, such as lakes, and on the floors of swamps. Accumulations of sand in beaches and dunes may eventually be transformed into sedimentary rock if conditions are right.

▲ These rock strata in Capitol Reef National Park in Utah were originally formed over millions of years when the area was at the bottom of a sea. Later, uplift of land and erosion resulted in the formations that exist today.

Putting Sedimentary Rocks to Work

When trying to list the most useful sedimentary rocks, coal may be the first thing that comes to mind. There are, however, many others. Sedimentary rocks are the source of such fossil fuels as oil and natural gas. Conglomerate and other sedimentary rocks play a major role in the construction industry. Limestone is used to make cement. Shale is also sometimes used to make cement, as well as bricks. Limestone and sandstone are important building stones. There are many examples outside the construction industry as well. Gypsum is used as an ingredient in making various products, such as plaster of paris, pottery, and cake icing. Rocks containing phosphate are used to make fertilizer. Rock salt is a primary source of salt, which is an essential component of our diet and is also used for many purposes. (Salt is also produced through the evaporation of seawater.)

Sedimentary rocks can tell scientists a lot about the past. The rocks' makeup carries clues about the conditions that existed when the rocks were created. Sediment tends to be laid down in layers, or strata. This layering helps scientists identify neighboring areas of rock that were formed at the same time.

Sedimentary rocks also give clues about life in the distant past. These clues usually involve fossils, which are remains or traces (such as tracks or burrows) of ancient living things. Fossils often form part of the materials found in sedimentary rock.

Types of Sedimentary Rocks

Sedimentary rocks can be divided into three types. They are called clastic, chem-ical, and organic (or biological). The basic difference between these types is the way they were formed. This results in differences in appearance.

Clastic comes from the Greek word *klastos,* meaning "broken." Clastic rocks are made from broken pieces of other rocks. For example, sand grains are tiny bits of rock. If these bits are squeezed together long and hard enough, the result is the clastic rock called sandstone.

The bits of material in silt or mud are extremely tiny. If they are pressed tightly enough together to form a rock, the result is shale or mudstone. Shale and mudstone are rather soft and have finer grains than sandstone.

Clastic rocks may contain rock pieces that are bigger than sand grains. The

pieces may even be as big as boulders! Smaller bits of material help to cement these pieces together. If the pieces have spent a long time in moving water, they will have rounded edges. The same is true of pieces that have been moved and tumbled a lot among other rocks. Sedimentary rocks containing such smooth-edged pieces are called conglomerates. If the original rock pieces were simply piled up at the foot of a mountain, however, their edges will be sharp. The sedimentary rock containing them is called breccia.

▲ Sandstone can sometimes take rather impressive shapes and sizes.

Chemical rocks contain principally material that was carried or dissolved in water. Under certain conditions, the material settles on the bottom of the body of water, where it may form solid crystals. Another way dissolved material may separate, or precipitate, from water is to be left behind when the water evaporates. Examples of rocks formed by precipitation from water include rock salt (halite), rock gypsum, a few types of limestone, and most of the world's important

iron ore deposits. In caves, stalactites and stalagmites are formed from minerals in dripping water. Stalactites look like icicles and extend from the roof of a cave. Stalagmites are deposits that build up from the floor.

Organic rocks form mainly from the remains of living things. Among the types of remains that may end up in

▲ You can see some of the variety of sedimentary rocks in these examples. Conglomerate *(left)* is a clastic rock containing rock pieces that tend to be smooth or rounded. The pieces in breccia *(center)*, a different sort of clastic rock, are sharp edged. Some limestones *(right)* contain an abundance of fossils.

Evaporites

Sometimes conditions are such that the water in a shallow sea or other body of water evaporates at a relatively fast rate. Still, that process may take thousands of years. If the sea gets cut off from its source of water, it may even completely dry up. The minerals dissolved in the water precipitate out and are left behind, forming a type of chemical sedimentary rock called an evaporite. Thick beds of rock salt are formed in this way. Evaporites can be useful sources of other minerals as well, depending on what was in the water before evaporation. Gypsum is mined from evaporite beds. Evaporites are also sources of nitrates, which are used in fertilizers and explosives. These salt flats *(above)* at Death Valley, California, are evaporite deposits.

organic rocks are plants, shells, bones, and the skeletons of tiny living organisms called plankton. Lignite and bituminous coal, for example, develop from ancient plant remains. Limestone comes mainly from the shells of tiny creatures living in reefs or on the sea bottom. Chalk is a soft type of limestone.

Metamorphic Rocks

The word *metamorphism* means "change of form." Metamorphic rocks are rocks that have changed as a result of being subjected to new conditions. These conditions may involve increased heat, increased pressure, or exposure to fluids containing substances that can help alter the rock's makeup. (For example, hot water sometimes carries certain chemicals, such as carbon dioxide, that may dissolve material in the rock, cause chemical reactions, or promote the formation of crystals.) Most often the new conditions involve heat and/or pressure that bakes the original rock. However, the combined effect must not be so great as to cause the original rock to melt. If the original rock melts, it becomes magma. When it cools, the new rock is considered igneous rather than metamorphic.

Metamorphism changes any kind of rock—igneous, sedimentary, or metamorphic—into a new metamorphic rock. Metamorphic rocks have some things in common. They are usually harder than the original rock. Also, they contain crystals. The kinds of changes that happen in metamorphism depend on the makeup of the original rock and on the conditions the rock undergoes. Metamorphism may alter the rock's crystal pattern or texture, for example, or it may change the original minerals into different ones.

Contact and Regional Metamorphism

When scientists talk about metamorphism, they commonly have in mind effects caused by heat or pressure. There are two chief ways such metamorphism can take place. One is called contact metamorphism. This can occur when a bit of rock comes into contact with hot flowing magma or lava. The amount of rock affected is small. Contact metamorphism can happen at the surface, since hot lava appears there. Usually, however, the conditions causing it are found somewhere deep underground.

Another way rock changes is called regional metamorphism. Large amounts of rock are exposed to high pressure or heat below the surface. This kind of metamorphism can happen, for example, below a mountain range, whose weight subjects the rock below it to high pressure. High pressure and heat can also occur as a result of major rock movements. The outer layer of Earth is broken up into a number of large slabs called tectonic plates. Some are under continents, and some are under oceans. Forces from deep below the plates cause them to move slowly. In some places, plates slip past each other. In some places, they bang into each other. The edge of one plate may be pushed under another, exposing rocks at the edge to the high heat that exists deep below. One way or another, rocks in a large region are exposed to enough heat and pressure to undergo change.

Foliation

Because of the pressure they undergo, the crystal grains in regional metamorphic rocks are often arranged in parallel stripes or flat sheets. This is called foliation. In a way, it is like the grain pattern in wood. Schist and gneiss are common regional metamorphic rocks that show obvious foliation. They form under high pressure and at high temperatures, and they have coarse grains. Slate forms from the sedimentary rock shale under more moderate conditions. It has fine grains and can easily be split into sheets. Marble usually forms from limestone. It has an even texture and lacks foliation.

Foliation ordinarily does not occur in contact metamorphic rocks. The most

▲ Some metamorphic rocks are foliated. They appear to be made of layers. Some are not foliated. This gneiss in Bayerischer Wald National Park in Germany *(left)* is an example of a foliated rock. The fractured quartzite in the Negev Desert in Israel *(right)* is unfoliated.

common contact rock called hornfels, for example, lacks foliation. Instead, it has grains to form even texture.

Getting to the Surface

Most metamorphic rocks are formed deep underground, so it may seem strange that they are often found on the surface. How does this happen? Sometimes forces within Earth lift up sections of buried rock.

Metamorphic rocks also can reach the surface as a result of erosion, when rock and soil that cover metamorphic rocks are worn away. Thanks to these natural processes, many metamorphic rocks are available for a variety of purposes. Scientists value these rocks because they carry clues about their origins. They reveal what conditions are like deep within Earth's crust.

Putting Metamorphic Rocks to Work

Marble has a smooth texture, and the best-known type is white. Marble is also easy to carve, compared with many other rock materials. Because of features like these, it has been used for centuries to make statues and impressive buildings, such as the Lincoln Memorial in Washington, DC, with its seated statue (right) of Abraham Lincoln, the sixteenth President of the United States. Another well-known marble building is the ornate Taj Mahal in Agra, India.

Slate is another important construction rock. It is used as a finishing stone for buildings and as a material for roofing tiles and pool tables. Schist and gneiss are also used as building stones.

Anthracite, a hard, black coal formed from bituminous ("soft") coal by metamorphic processes, is an important fuel.

IN THIS TEMPLE
AS IN THE HEARTS OF THE PEOPLE
FOR WHOM HE SAVED THE UNION
THE MEMORY OF ABRAHAM LINCOLN
IS ENSHRINED FOREVER

③ ROCK CHANGES

Constant Activity

With rocks, change is always going on. New rocks are constantly being created on Earth. Right now, metamorphism is occurring all over the world. Hot lava is cooling into new igneous rock. Sediments are hardening into new sedimentary rock.

Meanwhile, many old rocks are under-going various kinds of changes. Some may gradually wear away, or erode. Others may be broken up by the growth of tree roots. Some may slowly break up as a result of weathering. Weathering includes various processes. Rocks may be eaten away by chemicals, such as acid in rainwater or in substances from living creatures. Rocks may also be slowly

▲ Horseshoe Bend in Arizona vividly shows the power of erosion. The Colorado River has carved a spectacularly curvy path through the rock.

broken down by changes in temperature, by freezes and thaws.

Movement on Earth's surface is another major cause of change in rocks. Glaciers, rivers, and landslides move rocks from one place to another. In the process, the rocks are knocked around and break up. Alternatively, they may end up in a place where conditions, such as temperature and pressure, are quite different. Movements below the surface of Earth also cause change. Rocks may be affected by the flow of magma from one place to another. The movements of the tectonic plates lift up land in some places, creating mountains, and cause land to sink in other areas. Earthquakes involve sudden movements of huge masses of rock. Some rocks may be altered by the new conditions they end up in. Some may be destroyed by the shock of the quake.

▼ Mount Belukha, located near Russia's border with Kazakhstan, is the highest peak of the Altai Mountains. The movement of mountain glaciers can drag rocks from one place to another

The Rock Cycle

Earth is more than 4 billion years old. For virtually this entire time, it has consisted of more or less the same amount of matter. (Meteorites and other objects coming from space have added some, but the amount is small.) As we have seen, rocks are constantly undergoing change. At the same time that old rock is being destroyed, new rock is being created. The old rock is recycled to make new rock. Scientists call this process the rock cycle.

To see how the process works, start at any part of the cycle and follow it step by step. Let's begin with hot magma. Suppose the magma moves into a cooler underground region or erupts onto the surface. It then cools off and forms igneous rock. Underground igneous rock may be brought to the surface. It might be carried there by movements in Earth's crust. It might end up there because the rock and soil above it were worn away. Igneous rock can even form on the surface, when lava cools. No matter how it gets there, igneous rock on the surface undergoes erosion and weathering. These processes slowly break it down into tiny pieces. The pieces may be carried away, perhaps to the sea. When a lot of this material

collects as sediment in one place, the pressure on the lower part of the sediment may be great enough to turn it into sedimentary rock. If the sedimentary rock happens to undergo high heat and pressure underground, it turns into metamorphic rock. The metamorphic rock may come into contact with very hot magma; it may be crushed between tectonic plates. It might be pushed deep into Earth, where it is extremely hot. Any of these events could make the

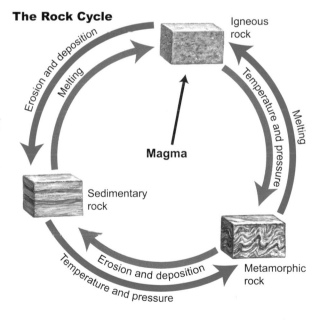

The Rock Cycle

Erosion and deposition

Melting

Igneous rock

Temperature and pressure

Melting

Magma

Sedimentary rock

Temperature and pressure

Erosion and deposition

Metamorphic rock

▲ The three basic types of rock—igneous, sedimentary, and metamorphic—are interrelated. Rock of each type can be turned into one of the other types. Scientists call this interrelationship the rock cycle.

A Complex System

The rock cycle is a perfect example of how Earth's parts are interconnected. The constant recycling of rock plays a role in two other important cycles, and they play a role in the rock cycle. Those two are the water cycle and the carbon cycle.

The water cycle is the constant circulation of water between the atmosphere and the surface of Earth. Water falls as rain and snow, and it evaporates back into the air, where it forms clouds, which eventually yield rain and snow again. Water helps break down rocks into tiny pieces, and moving water helps carry the pieces to places where the pieces can pile up as sediment and form sedimentary rock. These places are often within bodies of water. One way the rock cycle affects the water cycle is through the uplift of rock to form mountains. Mountains block winds, thereby helping make rain or snow fall.

The carbon cycle involves the circulation of the element carbon. All living things contain carbon. Carbon is also in the common gas carbon dioxide. Animals release the gas into the air when they breathe, and plants take it from the air for use in photosynthesis, the process by which they get sunlight to make food. Organic sedimentary rocks, which are formed from living things, contain carbon. Carbon is an important component of such common sorts of rock as limestone and marble, as well as coal. When these rocks are destroyed—limestone and marble by weathering, coal by burning—carbon dioxide may accumulate and may be released back into the air. Then the cycle begins again.

metamorphic rock melt and become magma. Then, the cycle can begin again.

Actually there is more to the cycle. Rock of each type can be turned into one of the other types. Rock of each type can also be turned into new rock of the same type. Any rock exposed to sufficient heat and pressure can melt. This means that under the right conditions, igneous and sedimentary rock can be turned directly into magma. When the magma cools, new igneous rock results. Also, erosion and weathering can affect any type of rock, not just igneous. Thus, under the right conditions, metamorphic and sedimentary rock may be broken down to form sediment. This sediment may accumulate and may eventually form new sedimentary rock. In addition, sedimentary rock is not the only type that can undergo metamorphism. Under the right conditions, igneous and metamorphic rock can also be changed into new metamorphic rock.

Layers Upon Layers

Sediment usually accumulates on a flat surface. As conditions change over time, the sediment may change in content or in the rate at which it is deposited. When sedimentary rock eventually forms, these differences in sediment give the rock a layered look. The layers, or strata, can be easily seen when something exposes them to view. For example, erosion by a river may create a canyon in whose walls sedimentary layers are visible. Road builders cutting through rock also may expose sedimentary strata.

▶ Rock strata occasionally are vertical rather than horizontal.

▲ These rock strata have been shaped into a vertical position by forces within the Earth.

▲ These curving strata are at the foot of the Hajar Mountains on the Musandam Peninsula in Oman.

The thickness and makeup of the strata in a particular area can tell geologists much about what happened there in the past. The strata's makeup may include not only minerals but also fossils of ancient living creatures. Scientists often find similarities between certain strata in different parts of the world. This may mean the strata were formed at the same time. By studying such strata and fossils found in them, geologists sometimes can discover what conditions were like over a wide area of the world at that time.

Two Basic Principles

A couple of basic principles guide geologists in their work. One is called superposition. This is the idea that in a stack of rock layers, the higher strata tend to be younger than the lower ones. So as you go lower, you go farther back in time.

Another basic principle is called original horizontality. This means that when sediments were originally laid down, they formed flat layers approximately parallel to the surface of Earth.

Although these two principles are helpful, geologists usually need more information to understand a series of layers. Over millions of years, many events might interfere with sedimentary strata. For example, a flow of magma might make its way into the layers.

Another possible event is an earthquake, which might cause a break in the strata, shifting one section in one direction and a neighboring section in the opposite direction. Such a break, or fracture, is known as a fault.

Also, pressure within Earth might cause the layers to tilt or even bend into a fold. The layers are no longer horizontal—a telltale sign of movement, according to the principle of horizontal originality.

Some Common Types of Faults

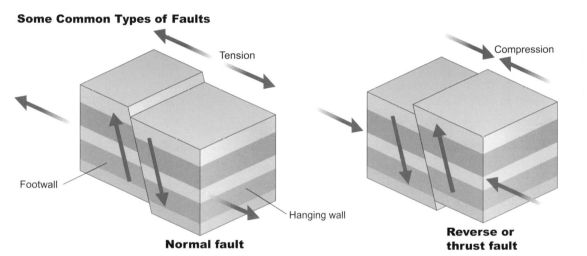

Tension

Footwall

Hanging wall

Normal fault

Compression

Reverse or thrust fault

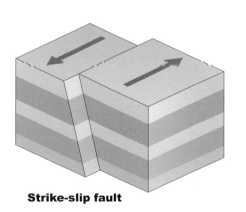

Strike-slip fault

▲ Forces in the Earth's crust can cause movement of rock along a fault, which is commonly at an incline. Faults are classified by the direction of this movement. In a normal fault, the blocks of rock on each side of the break are pulled apart by tension forces, and the block overlying the break—called the hanging wall—moves downward relative to the other block—the footwall. If compression forces are involved, however, the blocks are pushed together, and the hanging wall moves upward relative to the footwall. In this case, the fault is called a reverse fault if the inclination, or dip, is greater than 45°; it is a thrust fault if the dip is 45° or less. In a strike-slip fault, the movement is horizontal.

▲ Geologists examine a superposition rock strata formation at Chah Bahar, in southern Iran. Older rocks lie beneath younger rocks.

Need for Caution

Geologists need to be cautious when they draw conclusions. It is possible for powerful forces within Earth to shift older strata on top of younger strata. In that case, the principle of superposition does not apply. An unconformity is another factor that can complicate the job of "reading" history from a series of layers. An unconformity is a gap in the series where some layers seem to be missing. The layer above the unconformity is much younger than the layer below it. There are various possible reasons for such a gap. One is that the missing layers were eroded away before new strata were laid down. Another possibility is that environmental conditions changed and, for a certain period, no sediment was deposited.

Strata Man: Nicolaus Steno

Danish-born Nicolaus Steno (1638—1686) is often called the Father of Stratigraphy. He introduced the two basic principles of rock strata—superposition and original horizontality. Steno was also an expert in anatomy—which may have helped him make a key early discovery about fossils. He was assigned the job of dissecting a shark that had been found. In studying the shark, he realized that objects then called "tongue stones," which occurred in certain rocks, were really the teeth of ancient sharks. His was one of the first solid claims that fossils were the remains of living organisms.

Be a Collector!

Geologists study rocks to determine the history of Earth, but you don't have to be a scientist to find rocks fascinating. They come in countless varieties. Many are beautiful. Some are ancient, hundreds of millions or even billions of years old. Some are virtually brand-new, freshly cooled from lava. Rocks become even more interesting when you think of the powerful processes constantly at work to create, change, and destroy them.

Those are just some of the reasons that many people enjoy collecting rocks. Collecting has an added plus—it doesn't have to be expensive. You can spend as little as you like. Nor does your collection have to be big. Putting together even a small collection can be great fun.

If you want to start a collection, a good way to begin is asking yourself what kinds of rocks you want to look for. The ones you collect are called specimens. Do you want to get specimens of all major rock types? Maybe you would prefer to specialize in specimens of just one type, such as igneous rocks. Would you like to put together a set of rocks typical of your area? Perhaps you simply like rocks that look weird.

Whatever your objective, you will need to make some decisions. Rocks are tough and don't need special conditions. Still, you will need to set up a place to keep your specimens. Shoeboxes and egg cartons will do fine. Be sure to have some way to keep track of your rocks. If each has its own container, you could write notes on a card kept with the rock. The kinds of things you write will depend on your interests and knowledge. Some people like to record, where possible, such information as the name of the rock, who found it, where and when it was found, and what the place was like geologically. Another method is to keep all your information in a notebook. Give each specimen a number, which can be painted on the rock. Then write your information, along with the number, in the notebook. With this approach, you don't need a separate container for each rock.

Geologic maps can be a big help in finding and identifying rocks. The leading source of such maps in the United States is the U.S. Geological Survey (www.usgs. gov/pubprod). Other things a collector may find helpful are a geologist's hammer and a simple pocket magnifier. You can use the hammer to break off a rock and trim it down to a convenient size. The magnifier will give you a close-up look at specimens.

If you are thinking of looking for rocks on private property, be sure to ask the owner for permission first. Also, don't forget that collecting rocks in national and state parks is generally illegal.

4 FOSSILS GALORE

What Are Fossils?

Fossils are traces or remains of living things that died long ago. Scientists use the word *fossil* for almost any evidence of ancient life that they find in the ground. Many fossils are themselves rocks. For example, a bone or other body part that has been turned into stone by chemical processes is a fossil. Also, a fossil is an animal footprint made in mud that later became sedimentary rock. Not all fossils are stone, though. Sometimes actual body parts survive. This happens most often with hard body parts, such as teeth, bones, and shells.

Fossils have been found that are only a few thousands of years old. Some living creatures have changed in various ways in the quite recent past—changes that scientists can track by studying fossil remains. Much older fossils have also

▼ Hard body parts, such as the bones shown here, are much more likely to be preserved as fossils than are the soft parts of an animal's body, which may leave only a hint of their existence, or nothing at all.

been discovered. In fact, scientists have found fossils from most of Earth's history. Among the oldest known fossils are sedimentary formations believed to have been made by tiny living things called cyanobacteria, or blue-green algae. These earliest fossils are more than 3 billion years old. This is just a few hundred million years younger than the oldest known rocks.

Fossils Far and Wide

Such extremely old fossils are rarely found. Fossils from more recent periods are more common, turning up especially in sedimentary rock layers.

Fossil Tales

People began finding fossils in the ground thousands of years ago. To many, the finds seemed to be just rocks with weird shapes. A few people thought some of the discoveries, such as shells, might be from past creatures. Even those who imagined that the fossils came from living things did not realize how old the fossils were. In most cases, people did not understand what kinds of creatures made the fossils. When huge bones were uncovered, they were thought to be from monsters or human giants. Not until the past couple of centuries or so did scientists begin to understand the true nature of fossils.

▲ The dark color near the top of this cliff in the Geikie Gorge on Australia's Fitzroy River is cyanobacteria, tiny life-forms that, like plants, can get their energy from the Sun via photosynthesis. The oldest known fossils include sedimentary structures called stromatolites, which are thought to have been made by cyanobacteria more than 3 billion years ago.

Fossils can be found elsewhere as well. For example, bits and pieces of amber, which is the fossilized resin from ancient pine trees, can be found in various parts of the world, especially along the coast of the Baltic Sea. Resin—which is the pitch or sap of the tree—is a very sticky substance. If an insect happens to get stuck in the resin, the parts of the insect's body that do not rot away may remain there while the resin hardens. Polished pieces of amber are popular gemstones.

▲ Several wasps once got caught in some sticky tree resin, which eventually turned solid, becoming the piece of amber shown here.

Geologists, however, are interested in amber more for the life-form remains it may contain than for its value as a gemstone.

The study of these and all other fossils is called paleontology. Paleontologists work to find out what life and the environment were like in Earth's past. This is an enormous job. The number of different kinds, or species, of plants and animals that lived in past times is huge. Many of them, such as dinosaurs, have died out entirely, and are known only by means of fossils.

Forming Fossils

Most living things that once existed disappeared without a trace. Relatively few left fossils. Conditions have to be just right for fossils to survive millions of years. The fossils that have lasted were well protected. They are usually enclosed in rock or a similar hardened material. Some of these hard items are trace fossils, left by a living thing in material that later turns into rock. For example, suppose a dinosaur walks across a beach, leaving footprints in the wet sand. Then suppose the ground gets covered up and eventually turns into sedimentary rock. If traces of the dinosaur's tracks survive, they are fossils. A burrow made by a worm and bite marks made by a dinosaur are also examples of trace fossils.

Sometimes a part of an animal or a plant becomes a stony fossil. To understand how this happens, imagine that a dead creature gets covered up with sediment. As sediment piles up, it slowly turns to sedimentary rock. Under certain conditions, minerals carried by water in the ground can replace materials in whatever body parts happen to remain. The minerals gradually turn into stone. When this happens, the body part is said to be "petrified." The original shape of the body part remains, but the material it was made of has been replaced. This process takes a very long time. Soft body parts of a dead living thing tend to disappear quickly. They may be eaten by animals or simply rot away. For this reason, most petrified body parts are hard parts, such as bones. Bones give us good clues, however.

▲ This impression made in sedimentary rock preserves the shape of a fish that lived long ago.

Fossil Pioneer: Louis Agassiz

Louis Agassiz (1807—1873) was a leading biologist and geologist of his day. Born in Switzerland, he moved to the United States in the 1840s and became a professor at Harvard University. Agassiz's research on fossils of fish and other sea animals led to the publication of several important books and helped attract many other scientists to fossil studies. He is also known as the Father of Glaciology. He made key contributions to the study of glaciers and was one of the first scientists to propose the theory of the Ice Age.

Complete and Partial Copies

In some cases, a petrified fossil is a close copy of the original living thing. Even the inside of the fossil may closely copy the original, although the inside is now made of different material. Petrified trees, such as those in the Petrified Forest National Park in Arizona, are good examples of this process.

In other cases, a fossil from a living thing may not be a full copy. Suppose a hard body part, such as a shell or bone, gets covered up with sediment and is then completely dissolved by water in the ground. Suppose, too, that its shape happens to get preserved in the sediment. If the space inside the shape is empty, the resulting copy is known as a mold. If the space happens to get filled with new material, the resulting copy is called a cast. Molds can form under other conditions as well. Most fossils in amber are molds.

▼ The Petrified Forest National Park in eastern Arizona contains many pieces of petrified tree trunks. The inset shows one piece up close. The fossil trees were left behind when the sediment that covered them eroded away.

Many plant fossils are also incomplete copies. When a plant leaf falls on the ground, it tends to decompose quickly. Sometimes, though, leaves get buried. Under the right conditions, a trace, or imprint, of the leaf may remain within the dirt. If the area gets covered with sediment, and if the sediment eventually turns into rock, the imprint may be preserved. The leaf itself has disappeared, except perhaps for some of the carbon in it. The imprint is a sort of mold fossil.

Unpetrified Fossils

Several kinds of fossils contain original material from a creature. Sometimes hard body parts are found that have not yet petrified. Sometimes a creature becomes trapped in a material, such as ice or frozen ground, that preserves some soft parts for a long time. The cold slows or even prevents decay. If an animal dies in an icy area and quickly freezes, its body may last for a very long time, especially if it happens to get covered up. In Siberia, Russia, dozens of elephant-like animals called mammoths have been found preserved in this way. The

▼ Remains of a mammoth discovered by two children near the village of Yukagir in Siberia, Russia, in 2002 were extremely well preserved, thanks to the region's cold temperatures. Shown here is the head of the huge beast, which lived perhaps 20,000 years ago.

mammoths lived during the Ice Age. That was a time when much of Earth was covered by big ice sheets. It ended about 11,000 years ago, and scientists believe the mammoths died out at about that time or soon after.

Chemical Fossils

One major group of fossils is hard to see because they are buried below Earth's surface or contained within rocks. Scientists, however, can use them to learn about the past. These are called chemical fossils. They are substances from ancient living things that scientists can identify in sedimentary strata.

Certain other substances thought to be derived from ancient living things play a very important part in modern life. These are fossil fuels such as oil and natural gas. Most scientists believe, that fossil fuels have developed from the decayed remains of plants and microorganisms that became buried under heavy masses of sediment. Subjected to high pressure and heat, substances in these remains underwent chemical changes that led to the formation of oil and natural gas. Plant remains that were buried under somewhat different conditions were transformed into the solid fossil fuel known as coal.

Evolution and Extinctions

Fossils discovered around the world have made it possible for scientists to create a picture of life in the past. That picture, however, is incomplete. For example, creatures with soft bodies, which easily decay, are not very likely to leave fossils behind. Most living things leave no trace of themselves millions of years later. Still, enough fossil finds have been made to put together a detailed picture for much of Earth's history. The fossil finds indicate that most of the species that ever lived on Earth have died out. Some scientists put the figure as high as 99 percent.

Study of rocks around the world indicates that environmental conditions have changed greatly during Earth's long history since its beginning. These changes include the makeup of the atmosphere, Earth's overall temperature, and even the locations and sizes of the continents and oceans.

Adding the rock data to information from fossil finds shows how evolution took place over hundreds of millions of years. As environmental conditions changed, some species died out. Meanwhile, others evolved into new types with characteristics that were better adapted to the new conditions.

Mass Extinctions

Fossil evidence also shows that at a few times in Earth's history, enormous numbers of species disappeared fairly quickly. These events are called mass extinctions. About 65 million years ago, for example, the dinosaurs died out, along with many other species, including the once-common mollusks known as ammonites. An even bigger mass extinction took place roughly 250 million years ago. By some estimates, more than 90 percent of all sea species and 70 percent of land species died out. This mass extinction marked the end of the trilobites. Trilobites were small, hard-shelled animals that lived on the seabed around the world. The huge group included thousands of different species. Trilobites existed for some 300 million years and left many fossils.

▼ Scientists have found fossils from thousands of different kinds of the little creatures called trilobites, which lived a few hundred million years ago. Some, like the one shown here, had their eyes on the ends of long stalks.

Looking for Fossils in Los Angeles

One of the richest sources of fossils from the Ice Age is in the city of Los Angeles, California. It's called the La Brea Tar Pits. Despite the name, the pits don't contain tar. Instead, they contain a sticky black substance known as natural asphalt. When animals and plants fell into the pits, they became stuck. Fossil remains of more than 150 types of plants and hundreds of animal species have been pulled out of the tar pits. The specimens died as much as 40,000 years ago. Among the most common animals found are thousands of dire wolves and more than 2,000 saber-toothed cats. Both species are now extinct. At the museum at La Brea, you can see statues like these mammoths that once lived in the area.

Scientists do not know exactly why the mass extinctions took place. It seems likely that they were set off by powerful shocks to the environment. It is not easy to say, however, what the shocks were. Perhaps a series of volcanic eruptions that changed the weather caused mass extinctions. Maybe radiation produced by a nearby supernova, or exploding star, was responsible.

Many scientists think the extinction of the dinosaurs was caused by global cooling that resulted when an asteroid or comet hit Earth and filled the atmosphere with dust.

Scientists have found a thin layer of the element iridium in sedimentary layers around the world that date from the time of the extinction. Iridium occurs much more often in objects from space, such as meteorites, than on Earth. Perhaps the iridium found in the thin sedimentary layer came from the dust formed by the impact of a large space object.

▶ An asteroid crashing into Earth—shown here as imagined by an artist—is one possible explanation for the mass extinctions that have occasionally occurred in the past.

5 DATING METHODS

To understand the history of Earth, scientists want to know which rocks or fossils came before others. They need precise information, such as when a given rock was formed. They want to know when a fossilized plant or animal was alive. Scientists use different types of dating methods to find the information they seek. Which method they use depends on the type of fossil specimen they are working with.

Relative and Absolute Methods
There are two general groups of dating methods: relative and absolute. Relative methods were developed first. They simply give an idea of whether one object is older or younger than another. Absolute methods came into use in the twentieth century. They use high-tech approaches to estimate an object's age.

The superposition principle plays a key role in relative methods. In a series of sedimentary strata, the layers that are higher up are usually younger. (Of course, this principle may not apply if forces within Earth altered the strata.)

Fossils found in newer, upper layers are probably younger than fossils found in lower layers.

Another major principle that helps scientists understand strata is called crosscutting. It says that if a change in strata is found, the change must be younger—that is, it must have occurred after the formation of the strata. For example, the existence of a fault suggests that an earthquake shook the strata. Any igneous rock that is present in the layers must have intruded into them after they formed.

Relative dating also makes use of fossils. If fossils of the same species are found in strata that are very distant from each other, this suggests that the strata may have formed at about the same time. This approach works mainly for fossils of species that did not survive very long. If a species survives with little change for an extremely long time, it may be difficult to link the species to a specific geologic period.

There are many kinds of absolute methods. They work in different ways.

Each can be used only on certain types of things. When several absolute methods can be used on a given fossil or rock, some are more accurate than others. The best-known absolute method is called radiometric dating. Certain types of materials, such as uranium, are radioactive. In other words, they give off radiation. Radiometric dating is based on this process.

Radiometric Dating

To understand how radiometric dating works, you first need to know that the atoms of some elements are naturally radioactive. That means that over some period of time (which may be short or

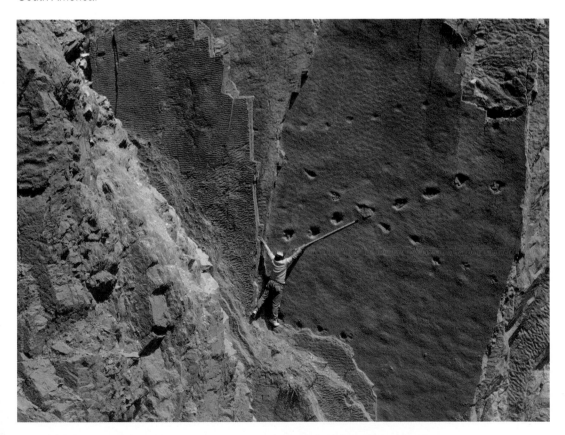

▼ The markings that this scientist is measuring are dinosaur footprints. They were made many millions of years ago on what was then a coastal area. The tracks were preserved as the ground was transformed into sedimentary rock and was gradually uplifted and tilted by powerful geologic forces. Today, the tracks lie on a nearly vertical slope in the Andes Mountains of South America.

long, depending on the element), an atom is likely to decay, or turn into an atom of a different element, called a daughter element. In the process of decay, the element gives off "radiation," typically a particle that constitutes a small bit of the original atom. Uranium, for example, eventually turns into lead through a series of such steps. For some substances, the process of decay takes millions of years. For others, it is much faster. Scientists know what these rates are for different substances. They estimate an object's age by measuring the amount of the original substance and the daughter substance it contains.

Radiometric dating can be used on a rock or fossil only if it contains enough radioactive material to be measured. Rocks and fossils usually contain just a tiny amount of radioactive elements, if any at all. Which radiometric method is used on a given object being measured depends on what elements the object contains. It also depends on whether the object is young or old. A method good for measuring ages in millions of years is of no use on an object that is only a few thousand years old. Likewise, a method that works well for short time spans is undoubtedly worthless for much longer periods.

X-raying the Past

It's easy to see how scientists can study the outside of a fossil. How do they find out what's inside, though? One way is to cut it open. This, however, may damage the fossil. Many fossils are delicate. To avoid damaging them, scientists sometimes use X-rays or other types of scans. X-rays and CAT scans done on people give doctors many different views of what is inside them. The same thing is true of fossils. Advanced X-ray methods such as CAT scans have been used to peer inside both plant and animal fossils.

Uranium methods are useful for objects millions of years old. A common method for objects that are much younger uses carbon-14, a radioactive form of carbon. This method, known as radiocarbon dating, can be used on fossils up to about 40,000 years old.

Chunks of Time

Finding out the ages of some fossils and rocks was a big step forward for geologists. They began drawing a picture of the history of Earth. Much is still unknown about Earth's past. New discoveries are being made all the time. Nevertheless, geologists have been able to put together a rather full picture for recent times. For the distant past, the picture is still hazy.

Almost 4.6 billion years have passed since Earth formed. Geologists divide this span into a four huge stretches of time called eons. The entire time preceding the eon we live in is sometimes called Precambrian time. It makes up nearly 90 percent of Earth's history. It covers three eons, but not much is known about them. The earliest eon is often called the Hadean. The name comes from *Hades*—or hell—many scientists think that conditions on Earth then were very harsh and quite unlike those that exist today. The oldest known rocks and minerals come from the Hadean. The next

▼ This exhibit from the New Mexico Museum of Natural History combines an artist's idea of life in the Age of the Dinosaurs with depictions of a few creatures' skeletons, as reconstructed from fossil bones.

eon is called the Archean, from a Greek word meaning "ancient." It is the source of the oldest known traces of life, such as the sedimentary structures called stromatolites that are thought to be formed by cyanobacteria. The following eon is called the Proterozoic, for "earlier life." The eon we live in began about 542 million years ago. It is called the Phanerozoic, meaning "visible life." Most known fossils date from this eon.

Eon Divisions

In cases where they have enough information, geologists divide the eons into smaller chunks of time. Some chunks are defined in terms of the life-forms that existed in them. Some are based on important geologic events. Eons are broken up into eras. Eras in turn are split up into periods. Periods are separated into epochs.

For example, our Phanerozoic eon is divided into three eras. It began with the Paleozoic ("old life") era. The second era was the Mesozoic ("middle life") era. We live in the third era, called the Cenozoic ("recent life").

The first period in the Paleozoic era is called the Cambrian. Because this period also begins the entire Phanerozoic eon,

earlier parts of Earth's history are called Precambrian. The Mesozoic era was the time when dinosaurs roamed the world. The most recent era, the Cenozoic, is the era about which geologists know the most. Even here, though, information is not complete. Geologists argue over how to divide up the era. It is usually split into two periods. According

Moving Continents

The continents are moving, but it is a very slow process. Major shifts in position take millions of years. Rocks and fossils are part of the evidence that this movement is taking place. In some areas, scientists have discovered fossils of animals or plants that require climate conditions much different from the conditions that exist in those areas today. Antarctica, for example, is now icy and supports few life-forms. At one time, its climate was warmer and life was abundant. Also, some areas that now lie on separate continents have very similar fossils and rocks. Once, these areas were next to each other. To understand this, look at a map of the world. Imagine moving South America to the east. Notice how nicely it fits into western Africa.

Moving Continents

225 million years ago

65 million years ago

Present

▲ The continents are slowly moving as a result of forces deep within Earth. Scientists think that at one time there was one large landmass. About 200 million years ago, it began to break up, eventually forming the continents we know today.

to a group of experts known as the International Commission on Stratigraphy (ICS), these periods are called the Paleogene and the Neogene. We live in the Neogene. It began about 23 million years ago.

Epochs usually cover several million years. The one we live in, however, is very short. Called the Holocene, it began just 11,000 or so years ago. It is the time of modern human civilization. The epoch just before the Holocene is also rather short. Known as the Pleistocene, it lasted a couple of million years or so. Huge ice sheets covered much of the world during the epoch. For this reason, it is sometimes called the Ice Age.

Geologic Time Scale

The Geologic Time Scale (see p. 44) shows the way many scientists today view the history of Earth. The scale is based mainly on information from the ICS. Some scientists do not agree with the way the commission classifies recent time. The dissenting scientists prefer to split the Cenozoic era into different periods: the Tertiary and the Quaternary. The Tertiary period is long. The Quaternary began only a couple of million years ago. It stretches up to today.

Geologic Time Scale

Phanerozoic Eon

Era	Period	When Began (millions of years ago)
Cenozoic	Neogene	23
	Paleogene	65
Mesozoic	Cretaceous	145
	Jurassic	199
	Triassic	251
Paleozoic	Permian	299
	Carboniferous	359
	Devonian	416
	Silurian	443
	Ordovician	488
	Cambrian	542

Precambrian Time

Eon	When Began
Proterozoic	3.2 billion years ago
Archean	about 3.8 billion years ago
Hadean	formation of Earth, nearly 4.6 billion years ago

Alternative View of Cenozoic Era

Period	When Began
Quaternary	about 2 million years ago
Tertiary	65 million years ago

6 BE A PALEONTOLOGIST!

What does a paleontologist do? Many options are available in this broad field of study! Some paleontologists work at digs—the sites where fossils are found. Others prefer to work in a laboratory, studying fossil specimens. A paleontologist may focus on one specific type of fossil, such as invertebrate animals or single-cell organisms.

Paleontology includes all sorts of branches. One studies the ecology of past times. Another looks at how fossils are made and preserved. Yet another focuses on how fossils are arranged in rock strata.

Most paleontologists are college professors. Others find jobs at museums. Still others are employed by the national and state governments. These scientists usually work in agencies connected with geology, such as the U.S. Geological Survey or geology-related state agencies. The oil industry is another career in which paleontologists work. Oil is a fossil fuel, and people who know about fossils can help search for the most likely places to find it buried.

To become a paleontologist, you need to go to both college and graduate school. In addition to courses connected with a particular branch of paleontology, other geology and biology courses are important.

If you think you might want to be a paleontologist, you can make a good start by getting as much experience as you can with fossils. One way to do this is by starting a fossil collection. Another way is to help out at fossil digs or at a local museum.

▼ Looking for fossils is painstaking work; even the tiniest specimen can be important. These paleontologists are at a dig, or fossil site, near Drumheller in Alberta, Canada.

GLOSSARY

atom A tiny particle that is the basic unit of matter; each element has its own sort of atom; atoms are the building blocks of crystals and other forms of matter

crust The thin, rocky outer layer of Earth

crystal A group of atoms that are arranged in a regular pattern

ecology The study of the relationships among living things and between living things and their environments

element A simple substance that has its own sort of atom; some of the most common elements in rocks are silicon, oxygen, and aluminum; carbon is an element found in all living things and also in many kinds of rocks that come from living things, such as coal

erosion The wearing away of rock or soil by wind, moving water, or ice (glaciers)

extrusive rock Igneous rock formed from magma that is pushed out, or extruded, onto Earth's surface

fault A break in rock strata that allows shifts in one direction or another

fossil A trace or remains of a living thing that died long ago

fossil fuel A type of fuel formed within Earth's crust from the remains of living things that died long ago; examples are coal, natural gas, and oil

gemstone A mineral or another substance (such as amber) that is highly valued because it is durable and can be cut and polished to have an attractive look

Geologic Time Scale A means of recording time since the Earth's beginning

geology The study of Earth and its history, particularly as shown in rocks

glacier A huge mass of ice that can flow downhill

grain A small particle of a mineral or other material in a rock; sometimes such particles

that are not in rock are also called grains, such as grains of sand

igneous rock Rock formed from the cooling of magma or lava

intrusive rock Rock formed from magma that has "intruded" into rock that already existed

lava Magma that flows onto the surface of Earth; rock formed from magma is also sometimes called lava

magma Hot, molten rock within Earth

metamorphic rock Rock formed from other rock that changes when it is subjected to new conditions, such as increased pressure or heat

mineral A solid substance made of one or more elements; the atoms of the elements form a crystal; many geologists also require that the substance be formed by natural processes, and not come from living things

paleontology The study of fossils and of life in past times as revealed by fossils

petrify To turn into stone

plankton Tiny plants and animals that live in the sea and other bodies of water

radiometric dating Some substances, such as uranium, give off radiation; radiometric dating estimates the age of an object on the basis of this process

sedimentary rock Rock formed as a result of the piling up of small bits of material called sediment

species A unique type of life-form, whether alive today or extinct

stone A piece of rock; the word is also sometimes used to refer just to rock material that is not metal

strata Layers, as of sedimentary rock

superposition A principle that in a stack of rock layers the higher strata will tend to be younger

tectonic plate A large slab of Earth's crust moved slowly by forces deep below eventually causing the development of mountains or mid-ocean ridges

texture The arrangement, shape, and size of the grains in a rock

trilobite A small hard-shelled animal that once lived on the seabed around the world

weathering The breaking down and disintegration of rock on Earth's surface by such processes as the action of chemicals (such as acid in rainwater), changes in temperature, and freezes and thaws

FURTHER INFORMATION

Books

Bonewitz, Ronald Louis. *Smithsonian Rock and Gem*. New York: DK, 2005.

Calhoun, Yael. *Earth Science Fair Projects Using Rocks, Minerals, Magnets, Mud, and More*. (Earth Science! Best Science Projects series). Berkeley Heights, NJ: Enslow, 2005.

Coenraads, Robert R. *Rocks and Fossils: A Visual Guide*. Buffalo, NY: Firefly, 2005.

Erickson, Jon. *An Introduction to Fossils and Minerals: Seeking Clues to the Earth's Past*. (The Living Earth series). New York: Facts on File, 2001.

Fortey, Richard A. *Fossils: The Key to the Past*. Washington, DC: Smithsonian, 2002.

Morgan, Ben. *Rock and Fossil Hunter*. (Nature Activities series). New York: DK, 2005.

O'Brien-Palmer, Michelle. *How the Earth Works: 60 Fun Activities for Exploring Volcanoes, Fossils, Earthquakes, and More*. Chicago: Chicago Review Press, 2002.

Ricciuti, Edward, and Margaret W. Carruthers. *National Audubon Society First Field Guide: Rocks and Minerals*. New York: Scholastic, 2001.

Web Sites

Mineral and Gemstone Kingdom
www.minerals.net

Mineralogy Database
www.webmineral.com

OLogy (American Museum of Natural History)
www.ology.amnh.org/earth/index.html

Rocks for Kids
www.rocksforkids.com

University of California at Berkeley, Museum of Paleontology
www.ucmp.berkeley.edu

Windows to the Universe
www.windows.ucar.edu/tour/link=/earth/geology/geology.html

DVDs

Rocks and Minerals, DK Eyewitness, 2006.

The New Explorers: Mystery of the Andes, A&E Home Video, 2006.

National Geographic: Dinosaur Hunter, National Geographic, 2003.

INDEX